D0744229

KIDS CAN COOK!

BACON ARTIST

SAVORY BACON RECIPES

EDGE BOOKS™

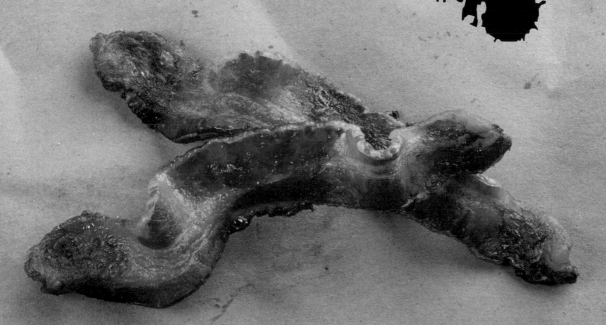

BY MARNE VENTURA

CAPSTONE PRESS
a capstone imprint

Edge Books are published by Capstone Press,
1710 Roe Crest Drive, North Mankato, Minnesota 56003
www.mycapstone.com

Library of Congress Cataloging-in-Publication Data
Names: Ventura, Marne, author.
Title: Bacon artist : savory bacon recipes / by Marne Ventura.
Description: Mankato, Minnesota : Capstone Press, [2017] | Series: Edge
    books. Kids can cook! | Audience: Ages 10–13. | Audience: Grades 4–6. |
    Includes bibliographical references.
Identifiers: LCCN 2016028372 (print) | LCCN 2016031736 (ebook) |
    ISBN 9781515738145 (library binding) | ISBN 9781515738268 (eBook PDF)
Subjects: LCSH: Cooking (Bacon)--Juvenile literature. | LCGFT: Cookbooks.
Classification: LCC TX749.5.P67 V46 2017 (print) | LCC TX749.5.P67 (ebook) | DDC 641.3/64--dc23
LC record available at https://lccn.loc.gov/2016028372

Summary
Easy to follow instructions and cooking tips teach young readers how to cook a variety of savory,
bacon-based recipes.

Editorial Credits
Aaron Sautter, editor; Sarah Bennett, designer; Laura Manthe, production specialist

Photo Credits
All photographs by Capstone Studio/Karon Dubke, Sarah Schuette, Food Stylist

Printed in Canada.
010021S17

TABLE OF CONTENTS

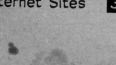

BECOME A BACON ARTIST!

Do you dream of the delicious, salty smell of sizzling bacon? Whether you like crispy bacon in a tasty BLT sandwich or savory bacon bits in cheesy potato soup, this book is for you. Learning to make your own snacks and meals is an important life skill. It's fun, and you can share what you cook with your friends and family. It's never too soon to start. Many of the world's greatest chefs began learning to cook when they were kids just like you.

SAFETY FIRST!

Cooking well requires a lot of care, which includes being careful around tools and equipment. Be sure to follow these simple rules to stay safe in the kitchen.

- Always ask an adult for permission to use sharp knives, hot stoves, and electric appliances. When in doubt, ask an adult to help you use them.

- Always cut your food on a cutting board. Avoid cutting your fingers by holding food with your fingertips curved inward. You should also always make sure that the knife blade points away from your body as you're cutting.

- Tie back long hair and tuck in loose clothing to avoid catching them on fire.

- Avoid spreading germs by always washing your hands with soap and warm water. Do this both before and after preparing food.

- Use dry oven mitts or pot holders to handle hot dishes, pots, and pans.

- Always wash fruits and vegetables before preparing them.

COOKING TIPS AND TRICKS

The best cooks usually have a plan in place before beginning any meal. Follow these tips in the kitchen to cook like a pro.

- Read all the way through a recipe before you begin. Then gather together the equipment and ingredients you'll need to make the recipe.

- Clear your workspace of clutter and keep the surface clean.

- Keep things simple by putting food and ingredients away as you work.

- Stay in the kitchen while you cook to avoid food disasters.

- Clean up completely when you're done.

TEMPERATURE

Fahrenheit	Celsius
325°	160°
350°	180°
375°	190°
400°	200°
425°	220°
450°	230°

PROPERLY MEASURING INGREDIENTS

- If possible, use transparent glass or plastic cups so you can check measurements at eye level.

- Measuring cups with a handle and spout are useful for liquid ingredients.

- Spoon dry ingredients into a measuring cup and level it with a knife.

- Measuring spoons are good for both liquid and dry ingredients.

MEASUREMENTS

1/8 teaspoon	0.6 gram or milliliter
1/4 teaspoon	1.25 g or ml
1/2 teaspoon	2.5 g or ml
1 teaspoon	5 g or ml
1 tablespoon	15 g or ml
1/4 cup	57 g (dry) or 60 ml (liquid)
1/3 cup	75 g (dry) or 80 ml (liquid)
1/2 cup	114 g (dry) or 125 ml (liquid)
3/4 cup	170 g (dry) or 175 ml (liquid)
1 cup	227 g (dry) or 240 ml (liquid)
1 quart	950 ml
1 ounce	28 g
1 pound	454 g

There is a variety of different types of bacon you can use in your bacon-based dishes. Smoked bacon is the most common, but you can use your favorite kind for most recipes. Become familiar with the following kinds of bacon so you know what to look for at the store.

Smoked Bacon — meat from a pig's belly. This meat is cured with salt and then smoked at a low temperature. This process helps keep the meat fresh longer than untreated pork. It also adds a tasty smoky flavor.

Slab Bacon — this large piece of meat is cured and smoked like regular bacon, but left unsliced.

Canadian Bacon — this type of bacon comes from the back of a hog. It's leaner than smoked bacon and is usually cut into round slices.

Pancetta — this Italian bacon is cured with salt but not smoked. It's often seasoned with pepper and other spices.

Turkey Bacon — bacon made from turkey meat and made in the same way as regular bacon. It is a tasty substitute for people who don't eat pork, or who want lower-fat bacon.

BACON COOKING METHODS

When cooking bacon you can simply throw it in a hot frying pan. But there are other ways to cook it that are healthier and leaves less of a greasy mess to clean up.

PAN FRY IT

- Lay bacon strips without overlapping them in an unheated skillet.
- Place the skillet over low heat and cover with pan lid to prevent splatters.
- Turn strips with tongs when they start to brown.
- Keep turning strips until they are browned evenly.
- Remove bacon and drain on paper towels.

MICROWAVE IT

- Place two sheets of paper towel on a microwave-safe plate.
- Lay up to four slices of bacon on the paper towel without overlapping.
- Cover with two sheets of paper towel.
- Microwave on high for about one minute per slice.

BAKE IT

- Line a baking sheet with aluminum foil.
- Place a wire rack on the baking sheet.
- Arrange the bacon slices on the rack without overlapping.
- Bake at 350° for 25–30 minutes.

MAKING BACON BITS

- Cook strips of bacon in oven, microwave, or skillet.
- Cool completely on paper towels.
- Cut cooked bacon into bits on cutting board, or crumble with clean hands.

BACON CHEDDAR DIP

MAKES 2 ½ CUPS OF DIP

If you're having friends over and want to serve up a tasty snack, then this cheesy dip will be a hit. Make up a bowl of this yummy bacon dip, add some veggies or your favorite snack crackers, and you'll be set!

INGREDIENTS

4 slices of bacon
2 green onions
1 cup shredded sharp
   cheddar cheese
2 cups sour cream
1 teaspoon dried parsley
¾ teaspoon ground
   black pepper
1 teaspoon salt
½ teaspoon garlic powder
¼ teaspoon onion powder
crackers or chips
fresh vegetables

EQUIPMENT

sharp cooking knife
cutting board
mixing bowl
mixing spoon

STEPS

1. Microwave the bacon and make bacon bits (see page 7).

2. Wash the green onions, and then cut off the root end. Finely chop up the rest of the onions.

3. Add all the ingredients to mixing bowl and stir until well blended.

4. Cover and refrigerate the dip for 24 hours.

5. Serve with crackers, chips, or fresh vegetables like carrots, cauliflower, or broccoli.

Try This!

Spread the bacon cheddar dip on flour tortillas. Roll up each tortilla and wrap in plastic wrap. Refrigerate for eight hours or overnight. When fully chilled, cut the tortillas into slices to make pinwheels.

BACON WRAPPED
MINI SWEET PEPPERS

MAKES 24 APPETIZERS

Your friends will think you worked all day over the hot stove to make these tasty appetizers. So don't tell them how easy these are to make. The colorful peppers and crispy bacon are delicious for the eyes as well as the taste buds.

DID YOU KNOW?
The average American eats about 18 pounds (8 kilograms) of bacon per year. The most popular meal for bacon is breakfast.

INGREDIENTS

12 colorful mini sweet peppers
8 ounces softened cream cheese
4 slices of bacon

EQUIPMENT

baking sheet
aluminum foil
wire rack
sharp cooking knife
cutting board
wooden toothpicks

Try This!

To add some heat, use jalapeño peppers instead of sweet peppers. Or for a seafood twist, wrap shrimp in bacon instead. Bake for about 20-25 minutes or until bacon and shrimp are fully cooked. Serve with sweet and sour sauce.

STEPS

1 Preheat the oven to 350° F.

2 Line the baking sheet with aluminum foil and set the wire rack on the baking sheet.

3 Wash the peppers. Slice in half lengthwise. Remove seeds and white membrane. Leave the stems on.

4 Fill each pepper-half with cream cheese.

5 Cut the bacon slices into thirds.

6 Wrap a bacon piece around each pepper-half. Secure the bacon in place with a toothpick.

7 Arrange the peppers on the wire rack with the cut side up.

8 Bake for 45 minutes or until the bacon is fully cooked and browned.

9 Cool for five minutes.

10 Remove the toothpicks before serving.

BACON DEVILED EGGS

MAKES 24 EGGS

Be a little devil by bringing these tempting deviled eggs to your next party. They are surprisingly easy to make and will keep well in the refrigerator for a day or two. However, they taste so good they probably won't last that long!

INGREDIENTS

12 eggs
4 slices of bacon
6 tablespoons mayonnaise
2 teaspoons prepared
  mustard
1/4 teaspoon salt
1/4 teaspoon pepper
smoked paprika

EQUIPMENT

large pot with lid
large bowl
sharp cooking knife
cutting board
medium mixing bowl
fork

STEPS

1. Place the eggs in bottom of the large pot.

2. Cover with enough water so that there's an inch or two of water above the eggs.

3. Bring the eggs to a boil over high heat.

4. Cover the pan tightly, turn off the heat, and let sit for 13 minutes.

5. While the eggs are cooking, microwave the bacon and make bacon bits (see page 7).

6. With a slotted spoon, move the eggs to a large bowl of ice water.

7. Peel the shell off the eggs. Then rinse under water.

8. Cut the eggs in half lengthwise.

9. Scoop the yolks gently into a mixing bowl and mash them with a fork.

10. Add the mayonnaise, mustard, bacon bits, and salt and pepper to the mashed yolks and mix well.

11. Fill each egg white half with about 1 tablespoon of the yolk mixture.

12. Lightly dust the tops of the eggs with smoked paprika.

DID YOU KNOW?

Bacon is high in saturated fat and sodium. Most health experts suggest eating a diet rich in fruits, vegetables, and whole grains. Bacon is delicious, but it should always be enjoyed in moderation.

Try This!

Peeling hard-boiled eggs can be tricky. To make peeling easier, crack the eggs several times against the counter. Then roll them around to loosen the membrane under the shell. The shells should peel off much easier.

BUNLESS BACON BURGER BITES

MAKES 12 APPETIZERS

These little burgers-on-a-stick are fun finger food for watching the game. If you have friends over, make a double-sized batch. These mouthwatering burger bites will still be gone by halftime!

INGREDIENTS

12 ready-made frozen meatballs
4 slices of bacon
3 slices cheddar cheese
6 cherry tomatoes
iceburg lettuce leaves
hamburger pickle slices
Thousand Island dressing
barbeque sauce

EQUIPMENT

baking sheet
aluminum foil
oven mitt or pot holder
sharp cooking knife
cutting board
large wood toothpicks
  or bamboo skewers

STEPS

1. Cover baking sheet with foil.

2. Place the meatballs on the baking sheet. Bake them according to package directions.

3. While the meatballs cook, microwave the bacon (see page 7). Cut each slice into thirds.

4. Cut the cheese slices into fourths.

5. Cut the cherry tomatoes in half.

6. Wash and separate lettuce leaves. Cut into bite-sized pieces.

7. One minute before the meatballs are done, top each with a piece of cheese.

8. Thread a toothpick or skewer through a tomato half, a lettuce leaf, a pickle slice, a bacon piece, and a cheese-topped meatball. Repeat to make 12 burger bites.

Try This!

Give your burger bites a Mexican flavor with pepper jack cheese. Skip the pickle slices, and dip the burgers in guacamole or salsa.

9. Serve the mini-burgers with the Thousand Island dressing or barbeque sauce for dipping.

BACON WEDGE SALAD

MAKES 4 SALADS

Salads don't always have to be a dull bowl of ripped up lettuce. Give your salad some character using a wedge of lettuce instead. With bacon bits, some ranch dressing, and cheddar cheese, this fun salad looks cool and tastes great!

INGREDIENTS

4 slices of bacon
1 tomato
1 head of iceberg lettuce
ranch dressing
1/2 cup grated sharp cheddar cheese
fresh ground black pepper

EQUIPMENT

sharp cooking knife
cutting board

STEPS

1. Microwave the bacon and make bacon bits (see page 7).

2. Wash the tomato and chop into bite-size pieces.

3. Cut the head of lettuce into fourths to form wedges. Place one on each plate, wedge side up.

4. Drizzle 2 tablespoons of ranch dressing over each wedge.

5. Top with tomato, bacon bits, and cheddar cheese.

6. Sprinkle with freshly ground black pepper to taste.

Try This!

Salads can be customized any way you want. You can add a creative twist with some chopped avocado, croutons, hard-boiled egg slices, or chopped red onion.

BACON WRAPPED
MAC AND CHEESE MUFFINS

MAKES 12 MUFFINS

If you like classic macaroni and cheese then you'll love this! It's quick and easy, and fun to eat. The smoky bacon flavor blends well with the cheese to make a mouth-watering dish.

EQUIPMENT

muffin tin
large saucepan
colander
small bowls
oven mitt or pot holders
wooden spoon or whisk

INGREDIENTS

12 slices of bacon
cooking spray
8 ounces of macaroni or other short pasta
1 tablespoon butter
1 tablespoon all-purpose flour
1 cup milk
4 ounces shredded cheddar cheese
1 egg
$\frac{1}{4}$ teaspoon salt
$\frac{1}{4}$ teaspoon ground black pepper
2 tablespoons dry bread crumbs
2 tablespoons grated Parmesan cheese

STEPS

1. Microwave the bacon (see page 7).

2. Spray the muffin tin cups with cooking spray.

3. Wrap a slice of cooked bacon around the inside of each muffin cup.

4. Preheat the oven to 400° F.

5. Cook the pasta according to the package directions. Drain in the colander.

6. Melt the butter in the large saucepan over medium heat. Add the flour and stir until mixed. Slowly add the milk, stirring constantly. Cook and stir for five minutes or until mixture is thick and smooth. Remove from heat, and then stir in the cheese until it's melted.

7. Beat the egg in a small bowl. Add to the cheese mixture, along with the salt, pepper, and cooked pasta. Mix well.

8. Fill the muffin cups evenly with about ¼ cup of the macaroni mixture.

9. Mix the bread crumbs and Parmesan cheese in a small bowl.

10. Spoon about 1 teaspoon of the bread crumb/cheese mixture onto the top of each cup.

11. Bake for 10–15 minutes, or until slightly brown on top.

12. Remove from the oven and let sit for 5–10 minutes before serving.

Try This!

You can try adding a colorful veggie twist to your cheesy muffins. Stir 1/2 cup of fresh or frozen peas, chopped broccoli, diced green chilies, or corn into the macaroni mixture before filling the muffin cups.

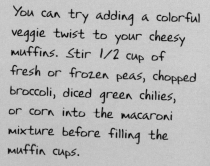

BACON CHEESEBURGER POCKETS

MAKES 8 POCKETS

These lip-smacking bacon cheeseburger pockets are sure to be a hit at your next party or game night. Serve them up fresh and hot out of the oven, or as a tasty, cold snack the next day.

INGREDIENTS

cooking spray
$\frac{1}{2}$ pound lean ground beef
4 slices of bacon
4 ounces shredded cheddar cheese
1 16-ounce can refrigerated biscuit
   dough (8 large biscuits)
barbeque sauce

EQUIPMENT

baking sheet
skillet
mixing bowl
sharp cooking knife
cutting board
oven mitt or pot holder

STEPS

1 Preheat oven to 350° F.

2 Spray baking sheet with cooking spray.

3 Brown and crumble the beef in the skillet. Drain any fat.

4 Microwave the bacon and make bacon bits (see page 7).

5 Mix together the cooked beef, bacon bits, and shredded cheese.

6 Cut a slit in the side of each biscuit to make a pocket inside.

7 Fill each biscuit with the beef mixture. Seal the edges tight.

8 Bake biscuits for 15-20 minutes or until golden brown.

9 Serve with barbeque sauce for dipping.

Try This!

For a lighter spin on this recipe, substitute shredded chicken for the ground beef. Then add 1/4 cup of ranch dressing to the meat mixture before stuffing the biscuits.

CHEESY BACON POTATO CHOWDER

MAKES 8 SERVINGS

What's better than hot soup on a chilly evening? You guessed it — cheesy soup with bacon! This hearty soup will help fill you up and has a pleasant bacon crunch.

INGREDIENTS

2 pounds frozen cubed
   hash brown potatoes
4 slices of bacon
4 cups chicken broth
1 cup milk
8 ounces shredded cheddar
   cheese, plus extra
salt and pepper

EQUIPMENT

large pot
colander
sharp cooking knife
cutting board
mixing bowl
large fork
oven mitt or pot holders

Try This!

Try adding some healthy green veggies to your soup. Add a cup of frozen peas or chopped broccoli to the potatoes during the last five minutes of cooking time. Or try giving your soup some zest by topping with sliced green onions.

STEPS

1 Put frozen potatoes in pot and cover with water.

2 Place over high heat and bring to a boil. Cook until soft.

3 Microwave the bacon to make bacon bits (see page 7).

4 Drain potatoes in colander.

5 Place 1 cup of cooked potatoes in a bowl and mash with the large fork.

6 Return both the mashed and cubed potatoes to the large pot.

7 Add chicken broth and return to a boil.

8 Reduce heat to medium. Stir in milk and cheese. Stir constantly until warm and thickened. Don't allow mixture to boil.

9 Add salt and pepper to taste.

10 Serve the soup in sturdy bowls with extra shredded cheese and bacon bits on top.

DID YOU KNOW?

Red potatoes are lower in starch than brown potatoes. They're good for soups, salads, and fried potato dishes. It's okay to leave the skin on because it's thin, soft, and full of nutrients.

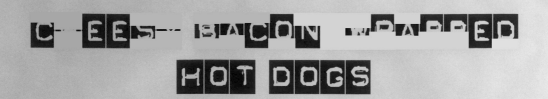

CHEESY BACON-WRAPPED
HOT DOGS

MAKES 4 HOT DOGS

What tastes better than a hot dog just off the grill? A delicious bacon-wrapped, cheese-stuffed hot dog — that's what! This easy recipe makes a great lunch or dinner.

INGREDIENTS

4 hot dogs
2 slices of cheddar cheese
4 slices of bacon
4 hot dog buns
mustard
ketchup
sweet relish

EQUIPMENT

baking sheet
aluminum foil
wire rack
sharp cooking knife
cutting board
oven mitt or pot holder
8 toothpicks

STEPS

1 Preheat your oven to 400° F.

2 Cover the baking sheet with foil. Place the wire rack on foil-covered sheet.

3 Cut a lengthwise slit down the center of each hot dog. To help keep the melted cheese inside, leave about an inch of the hot dog uncut at each end.

4 Cut the cheese slices lengthwise into fourths.

5 Insert two cheese strips into each hot dog slit.

6 Wrap each hot dog tightly with a strip of bacon. Overlap the edges of the bacon so the cheese won't melt out. Secure the bacon by poking wooden toothpicks through it and hot dog on each end. Remember to remove the toothpicks before serving.

7 Place on wire rack, slit side up.

8 Bake 35 minutes or until bacon is brown and fully cooked.

9 Serve hot dogs on buns with mustard, ketchup, and relish.

BLT SANDWICHES

MAKES 4 SANDWICHES

Are you tired of peanut butter and jelly sandwiches? Or maybe you're sick of the same boring turkey and cheese. It's time for some bacon! This classic bacon, lettuce, and tomato sandwich is a snap to make, and it tastes great.

INGREDIENTS

8 slices of bacon
2 medium tomatoes
8 slices of white sandwich bread
mayonnaise
4 leaves of lettuce
salt and pepper

EQUIPMENT

sharp cooking knife
cutting board
toaster

STEPS

1 Microwave the bacon (see page 7). Cut each slice in half.

2 Wash the tomatoes, then cut them into round slices.

3 Toast the bread.

4 Spread each slice of bread with mayonnaise.

5 Cover one slice of bread with a leaf of lettuce, 2 slices of tomato, and 4 bacon slice halves.

6 Add salt and pepper to taste.

7 Top with a second slice of bread and cut the sandwich in half.

Try This!

Make your BLT truly special by adding a fried egg, avocado slices, or a slice of cheddar cheese.

DID YOU KNOW?
People have been wrapping meat and cheese in bread for hundreds of years. It was John Montagu, the Earl of Sandwich, who gave the popular food its name in the 1700s. He asked for beef between slices of bread to eat with his hands, so that he could continue playing cards.

TWICE BAKED
BACON POTATOES

MAKES 8 POTATOES

Baked potatoes are a popular addition to many dinner plates. But they don't have to be a boring side dish. With some bacon, cheese, and sour cream, they can become the star of the show!

INGREDIENTS

4 slices of bacon
4 large russet potatoes
cooking spray
1 cup shredded sharp cheddar cheese, plus extra
$\frac{1}{3}$ cup sour cream
3 tablespoons butter
$\frac{1}{4}$ teaspoon salt
$\frac{1}{4}$ teaspoon pepper

EQUIPMENT

oven mitts or pot holder
baking sheet
sharp cooking knife
cooking spoon
medium-size mixing bowl
potato masher or fork

STEPS

1 Microwave the bacon and make bacon bits (see page 7).

2 Preheat oven to 475° F.

3 Wash potatoes and prick with a fork.

4 Place potatoes on oven rack and bake for one hour or until done.

5 Remove potatoes from oven with oven mitts and lower heat to 350° F.

6 Spray a baking sheet with cooking spray.

7 When potatoes are cool enough to handle, slice in half lengthwise.

8 Scoop out the middle of each potato half into the mixing bowl. Leave a ¼-inch (0.6-centimeter) thick shell.

9 Mash up the potato in the bowl.

10 Add bacon bits, cheese, sour cream, butter, and salt and pepper to taste to the mashed potato. Mix well.

11 Spoon the filling back into the potato shells.

12 Place the filled shells back on baking sheet. Sprinkle top of potatoes with extra shredded cheese and bacon bits.

13 Return potatoes to oven and bake about 20 minutes, or until golden brown on top.

Try This!

Add ¼ cup sliced green onion or ½ cup chopped broccoli to the potato mixture before stuffing the shells.

DID YOU KNOW?

Russet potatoes are great for baking or mashing. They contain more starch than red potatoes, which makes them light and fluffy.

BACON QUICHE

MAKES 8 SERVINGS

Quiche (KEESH) sounds like a super fancy dish. But it's simple to make, and can be served for breakfast, lunch, or dinner. Try this tasty bacon quiche when you want to impress your parents or grandparents!

INGREDIENTS

4 slices of bacon
1 small to medium onion
2 teaspoons olive oil
pre-made refrigerated pie
  crust in tin
1 ½ cups shredded
  cheddar cheese
salt and pepper
6 eggs
1 cup milk

EQUIPMENT

cutting board
sharp cooking knife
skillet
medium mixing bowl
whisk or fork

DID YOU KNOW?

Quiche originated in the northern Lorraine region of France in the sixteenth century. The word quiche actually comes from the German word 'Kuchen' or cake. The first quiches were single-crust pies filled with eggs and bacon.

STEPS

1. Preheat the oven to 375° F.

2. Microwave the bacon and make bacon bits (see page 7).

3. Peel and coarsely chop the onion.

4. Heat the oil over medium heat in the skillet and add the onion. Cook until the onion is soft and golden. Remove from heat and cool.

5. Sprinkle the shredded cheese evenly over the bottom of the pie crust. Add the bacon bits and cooked onion. Sprinkle with salt and pepper to taste.

6. Beat the eggs slightly in the mixing bowl.

7. Add the milk to the eggs and beat the mixture until foamy.

8. Add the egg mixture to the pie crust.

9. Bake for 45 minutes or until a toothpick inserted in the center comes out clean. Remove from oven and serve while still warm.

READ MORE

Cook, Deanna F. *Cooking Class: 57 Fun Recipes Kids Will Love to Make (and Eat!).* North Adams, Mass.: Storey Publishing, 2015.

Jorgensen, Katrina. *Food, Football, and Fun! Sports Illustrated Kids' Football Recipes.* North Mankato, Minn.: Capstone Press, 2015.

Sampson, Sally. *ChopChop: The Kids' Guide to Cooking Real Food With Your Family.* New York: Simon & Schuster, 2013.

INTERNET SITES

FactHound offers a safe, fun way to find Internet sites related to this book. All of the sites on Facthound have been researched by our staff.

Here's all you do:
Visit *www.facthound.com*
Type in this code: 9781515738145